TAMING THE OX OF THE MIND ESSENCE

Composed and Illustrated by
Oh All Wise One The Guru BAPR ALHF KM

ISBN: 978-1-4525-0606-7 (sc)
978-1-4525-0607-4 (e)

Library of Congress Control Number: 2012912254

Balboa Press books may be ordered through booksellers or by contacting:

Balboa Press
A Division of Hay House
1663 Liberty Drive
Bloomington, IN 47403
www.balboapress.com
1-(877) 407-4847

Because of the dynamic nature of the Internet, any web addresses or links contained in this book may have changed since publication and may no longer be valid. The views expressed in this work are solely those of the author and do not necessarily reflect the views of the publisher, and the publisher hereby disclaims any responsibility for them.

Any people depicted in stock imagery provided by Thinkstock are models, and such images are being used for illustrative purposes only.
Certain stock imagery © Thinkstock.

Printed in the United States of America

Balboa Press rev. date: 08/27/2012

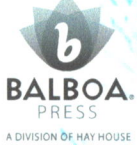

BALBOA
PRESS
A DIVISION OF HAY HOUSE

PREFACE

In China, an Ox represented the mind itself directly . . . not an idea about the mind, but the mind as it is.

The whole Universe is The Ox of our own pure mind.

This story, based on the twelfth century Chinese Ten Ox Herding Paintings, is about The World of The Mind.

Many of our Spiritual Masters have spoken about the importance of maintaining that original, pure, innocent child mind.

"Unless you become like little children (pure of mind) you shall not enter The Kingdom of Heaven"
Jesus

"Great is the man who does not lose his child mind"
Buddha

"Become as a little child, seeing all things for the first time."
Zen saying

Somewhere along life's journey we all set off on the pilgrimage of a 'Seeker'. Some find their way, some fall along the way, and yet others are lost before they even take the first step.

Peter Matthiessen, Muryo Roshi, in the following quote, has expressed so precisely the essence of the 'Seeker', first step (painting) in the story of the Ten Oxherding Paintings.

"Soon the child's clear eye is clouded over by ideas and opinions, preconceptions and abstractions. Simple free being becomes encrusted with the burdensome armour of the ego. Not until years later does an instinct come that a vital sense of mystery has been withdrawn. The sun glints through the pines, and the heart is pierced in a moment of beauty and strange pain, like a memory of paradise. After that day . . . we become seekers."

ACKNOWLEDGEMENTS

For this story, based on the twelfth century Chinese 'Ten Oxherding Paintings', I have referenced an internet site 'Commentary by Shodo Harada Roshi, May 1998. Much of the wording in this book was extracted from that source. The various quotes and 'Advice from . . . ' the characters portrayed in my version of The Ten Oxherding Paintings, are taken directly or loosely from our Spiritual Masters, Gods, Gurus, Buddhas, Roshis, Philosophers, Poets and Writers; and from Lewis Carroll's Wonderland characters, as we follow Alice's own journey to enlightenment.

DEDICATION

Oh Enlightened One Dharma Bum Mother Fay
With her creative contribution and computer skills, turned my scratching and scribbling into a book.

Mini-Me Guru Troy
For his painting "Taming the Ox of the mind essence."

Oh Enlightened One Dharma Bum Legend of the Universe 1st Marion
For introducing me to The Dharma Bums.

SEARCHING FOR THE OX

Standing at the foot of our mountain, young, armed with only a small pack . . . the knowledge that there is a path to be walked.

This realization that there is a possibility of reviewing our own behaviour, to want to change it, to work on our divine self, to make a difference, to seek the awakening of deep faith, the Bodhisattva Nature . . . only we humans can do this.

We are all searching for this deep mind . . . we are seeking.

Advice from Alice
Alice

"My journey has led me to this mountain; perhaps I should seek an easier path."

Advice from a Buddha
The Buddha

"The mighty do not go around."

Advice from a Chinese Philosopher
Confucius

"The journey of a thousand miles begins with the first step."

Advice from a Cat
Cheshire Puss

"Though we may take various roads, Alice, all are on the way. But beware! As soon as the path divides, you are lost.
Stay on the path."

Advice from a March Hare
Marchy

"Move Alice, and the way will open."

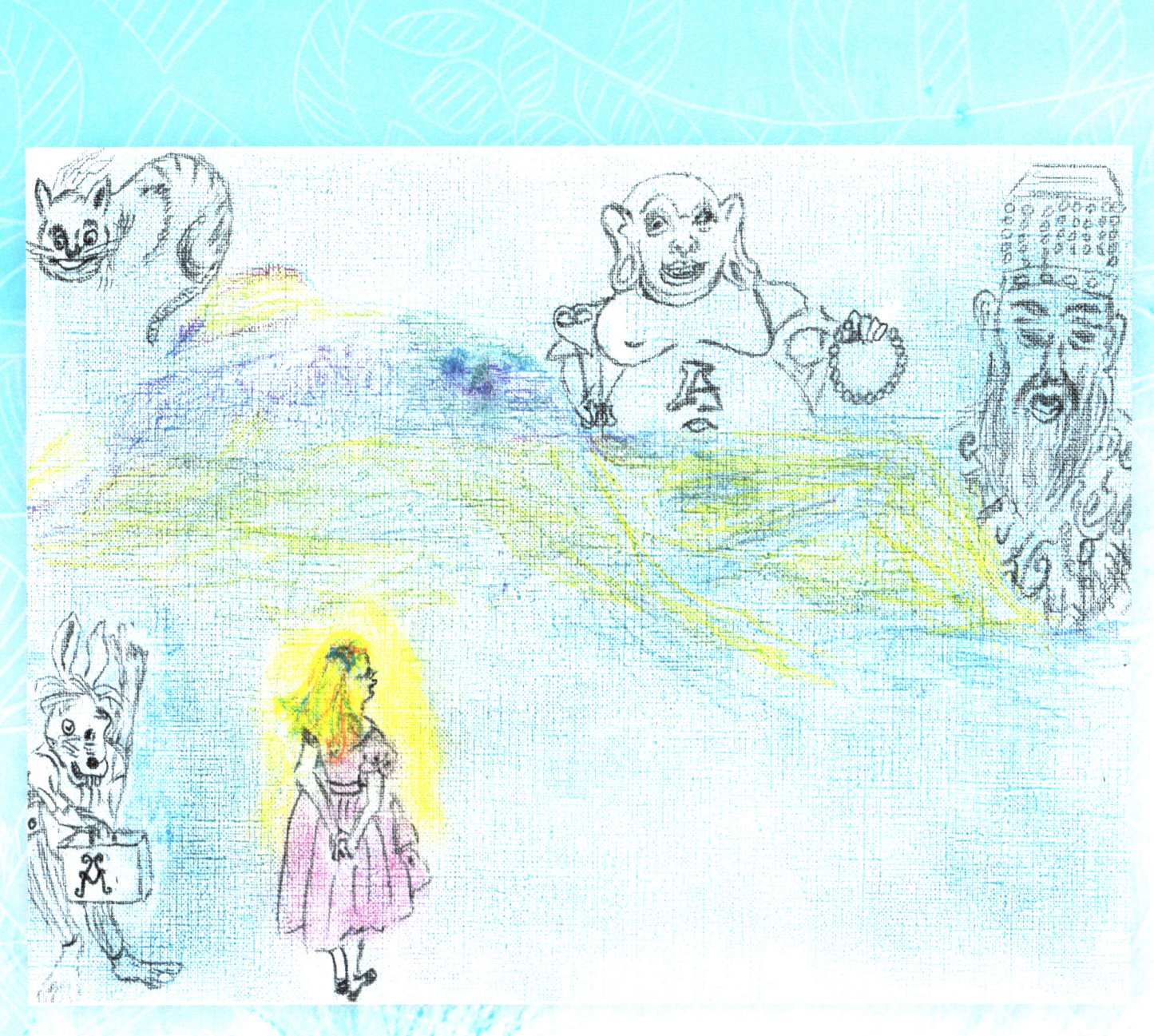

FINDING THE TRACKS

Seeking the path and the essence of that state of mind, finally something that looks something like a track is found. But this essence cannot yet be affirmed from one's own personal experience, only from reading and what has been learned. But it is sufficient for us to perceive a presence beyond the self, the presence of some other huge, great, enormous energy. Still for many, the journey becomes too burdensome as it seems the more we seek, the further away it goes. But for those who seek, the inspiration needed to stay on the path is omni-present.

Fair dinkum mate, if inspiration had teeth, it'd jump out and bite ya!

Advice from a Queen ***The Red Queen*** "There is no Cow of Enlightenment, not even a trace of a footstep. Off with her head!"	***Advice from Alice*** ***Alice*** "The Queen is awfully fond of beheading people...that can't be right...there must be a better way."

Never slacken effort, whatever the obstacle, however long the journey.
Swami Bhagawhan Sri Sathya Sai Baba

It is necessary to any originality to have the courage to be an amateur.
Wallace Stevens

Start a great project, and with the first step you will be amazed at the invisible forces that will come to your aid.
Deepak Chopra

Advice from a God
Jesus

"Seek and ye shall find, Alice. Knock and the door will open unto thee."

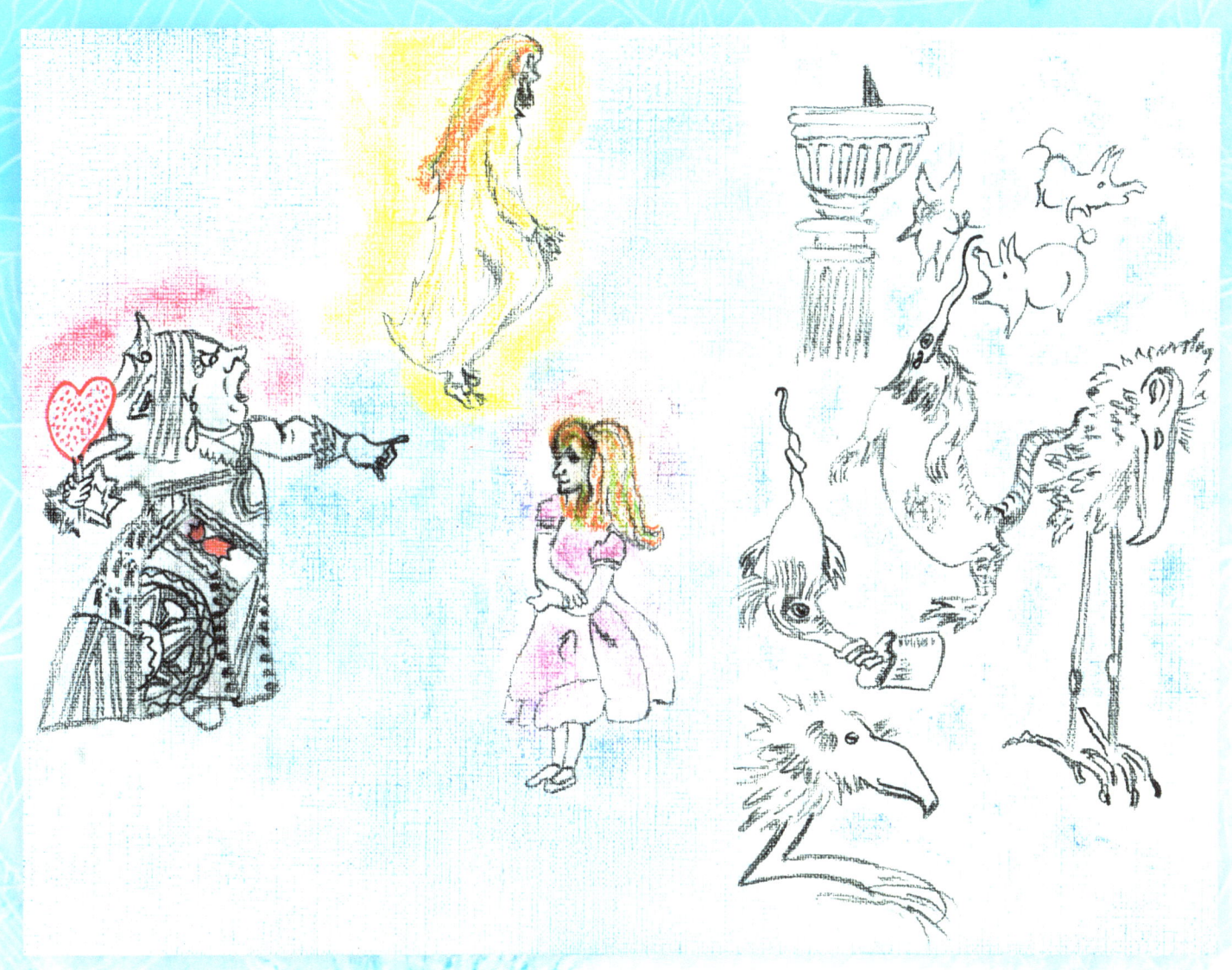

SEEING THE OX

Finally through our training, we have been able to see the Ox, but it is still only the rear end of the Ox, it's not clear. We need to meet the Ox directly. Beyond any ideas or dualistic experiences . . . Philosophers call this the pure experience . . . to know it from yourself completely.

On the tree branch a nightingale sings, warm sun, soft wind, green willows on the bank. Now, nowhere for it to hide, its majestic horns no artist could draw.

Advice from a Mock Turtle
Mockers

"With what porpoise do you go on this Journey, Alice? Why, when I was a real turtle and lived in the ocean, if ever a fish came to me and told me he was going on a journey, I should say, 'with what porpoise?' No wise fish would go anywhere without a porpoise."

Advice from Alice
Alice

"Perhaps it is my porpoise that has led me to the Jabberwocky, but I have only had a glimpse of the rear end. I hear that the Jabberwocky has very large, powerful horns, but as I have never seen it completely, I cannot honestly say what it even looks like. Perhaps when I meet the Jabberwocky face to face, I will then see my porpoise clearly."

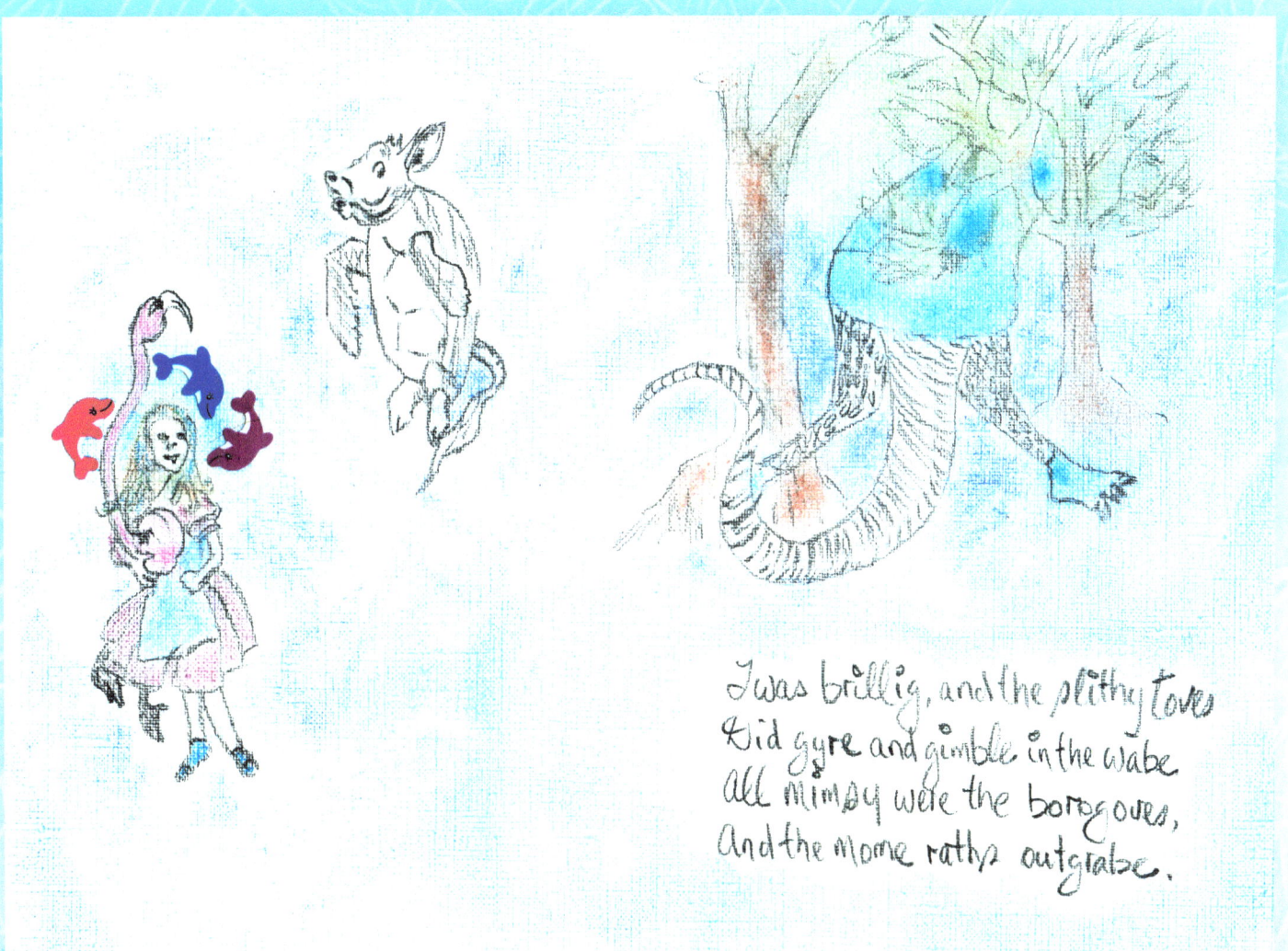

I was brillig, and the slithy toves
Did gyre and gimble in the wabe
All mimsy were the borogoves,
And the mome raths outgrabe.

CATCHING THE OX

At last you finally meet up with the Ox, so long hidden in the wilderness. But the Ox is just as wilful as before, and just as wild natured.

We have worked for years and realized something like an Ox.

We know it, but we cannot use it in our every-day lives as we want to.

As soon as we gain the high ground, it vanishes once more deep into the mist.

Catching the Ox is not about taking something or realizing something, but about letting go of everything.

Advice from a Rabbit
The White Rabbit

"Be tamed Beast! The Queen commands it."

Advice from a Jabberwocky
The Jabberwocky

"The Queen is off with her head.
I will not be tamed!"

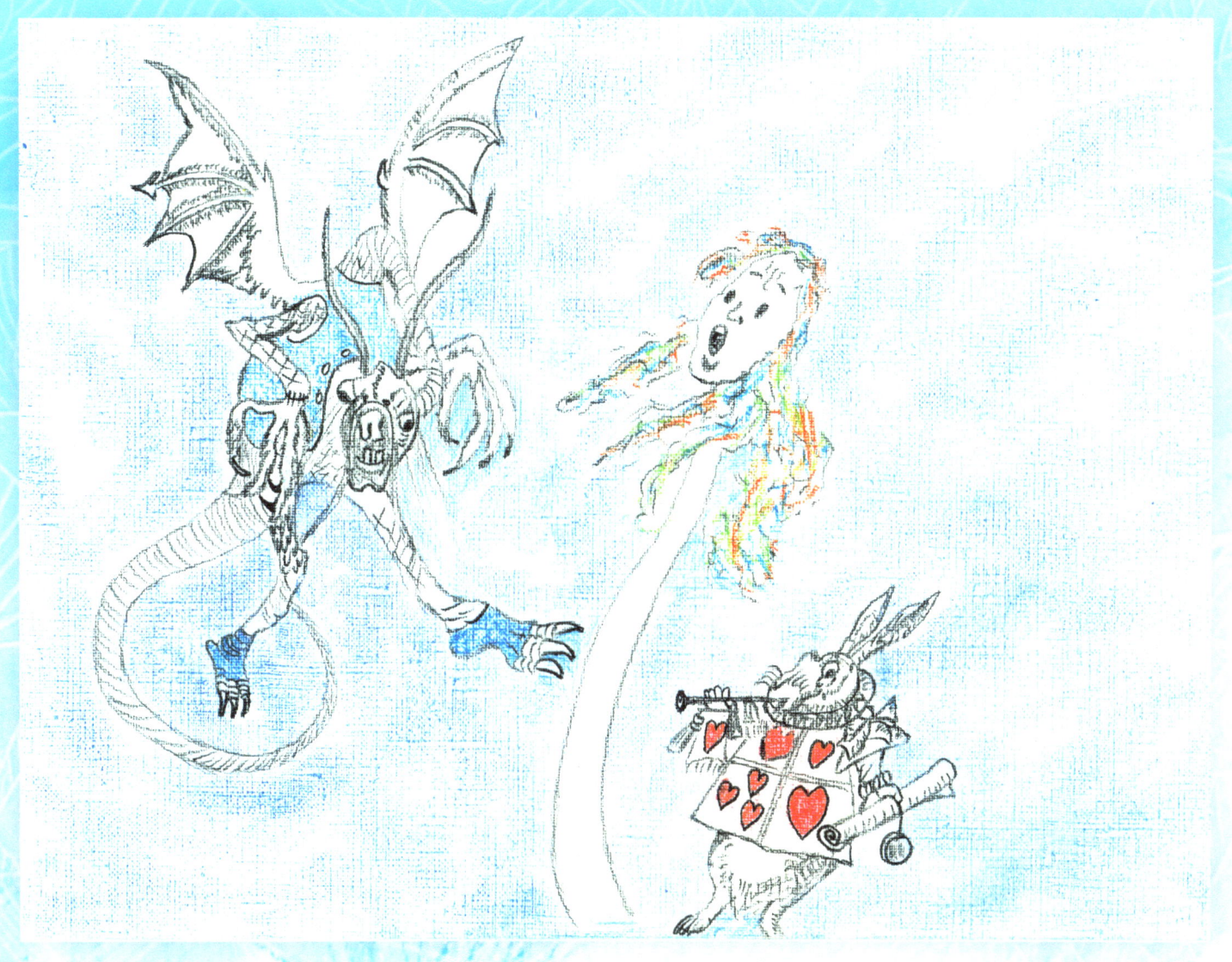

TAMING THE OX

To know that truly clear mind directly: This is taming the Ox.

Let drop neither whip nor line, even a moment, lest the Ox wander back to dust and desire.

Keep a firm grip on that rope and do not waver. We must touch that original mind directly.

We must actually know it from our own experience.

It is only because we know this clear mind that we can review our behaviour . . . This is taming the Ox.

We have been able to experience this essence, but not have been able to ripen it and keep it going.

We have to be able to tame the Ox as well as to have captured it.

With awakening, all becomes truth; but if you reside in ignorance, all is unreal.

Advice from a Guru
Swami Bhagawan Baba

"The war that goes on constantly inside us (the battle with the Ox)...once the battle is won, the victory needs a porpoise, a goal an, aim. Did you tame the beast, Alice, just that you might ride home on its back like some Queen?"

Advice from a Duchess
The Duchess

"She who knows does not speak, Alice.
She who speaks does not know.
Have more than thou showest.
Speak less than thou knowest."

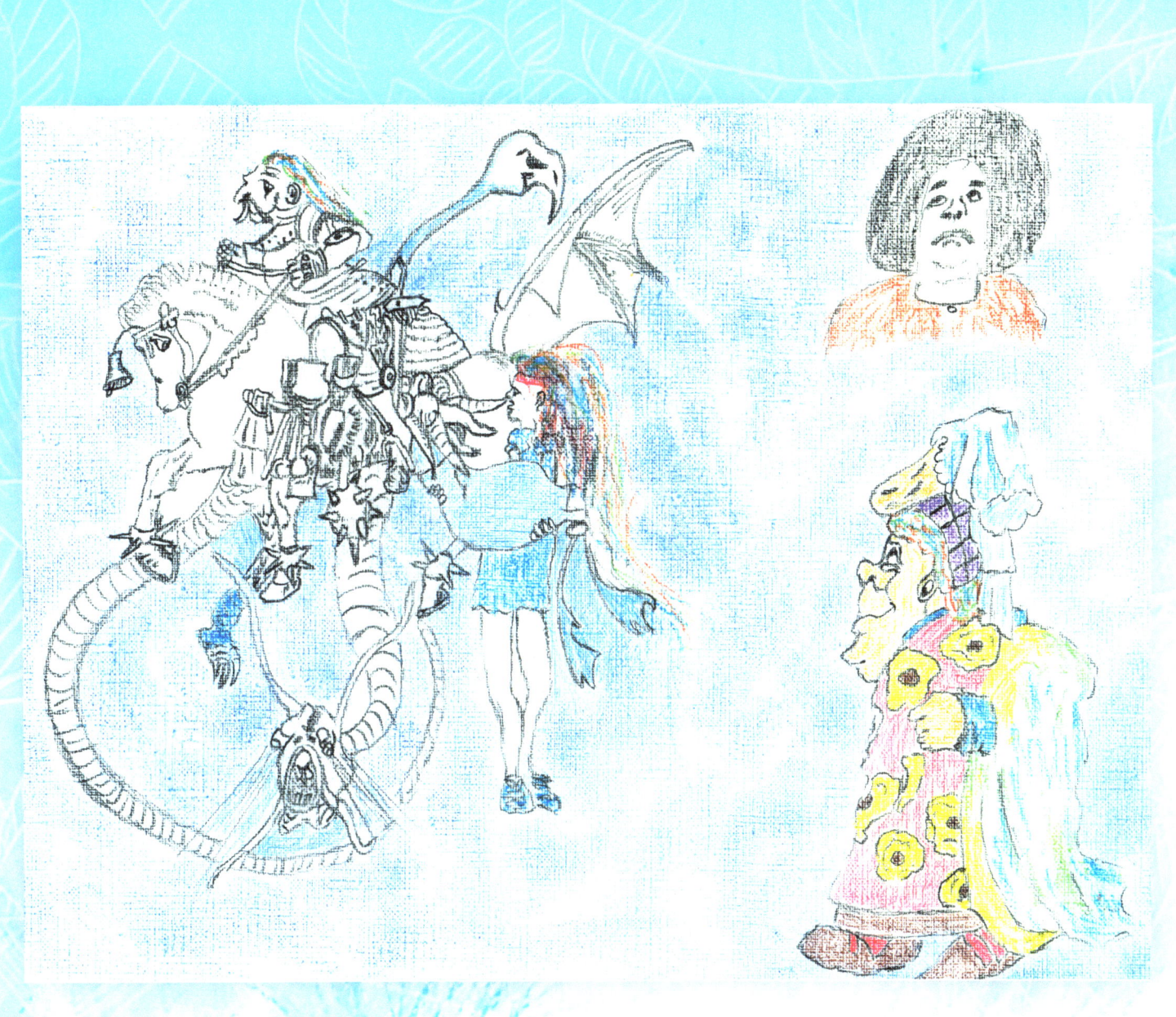

TAMING THE OX OF THE MIND ESSENCE

Meditate

Live purely

Be quiet

Do your work with mastery

Like the moon, come out from behind the clouds

Shine

Buddha

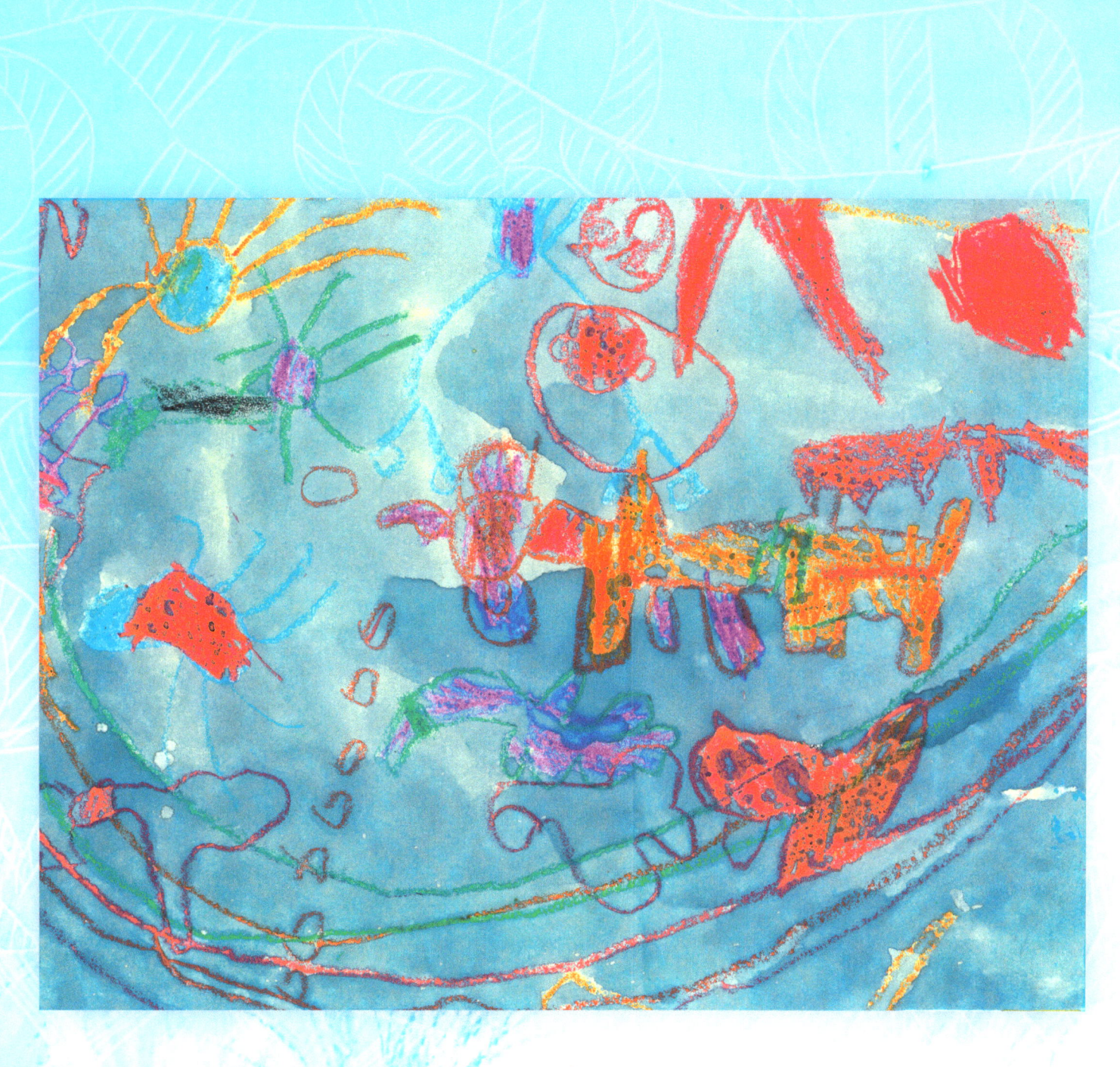

RIDING HOME ON THE OX

We have tamed the Ox and struggled with it, and now the Ox is facing the same way we are, and together we return home not even needing the reins any longer.

Lying back on top of my Ox, gazing at the sky . . . how gratifying

The realization that we have found the Ox; caught the Ox; tamed the Ox; we have let go of all sense of our 'small self'. It's as if we are riding peacefully for home on the back of the Ox.

Having come this far we are solidly in the world of *truth*. What we have achieved is an awakening to that state of mind that from the origin has had no problem and no obstruction and no delusion. This is a place that can easily be described as **'*every day is a good day*'** . . . our original essence,

but it is not easy to arrive there.

Advice from a Mad Hatter
Hatty

"Why is a raven like a writing desk?"

Advice from a cat
Cheshire Puss

"Every day is a journey, Alice, and the journey itself is home."

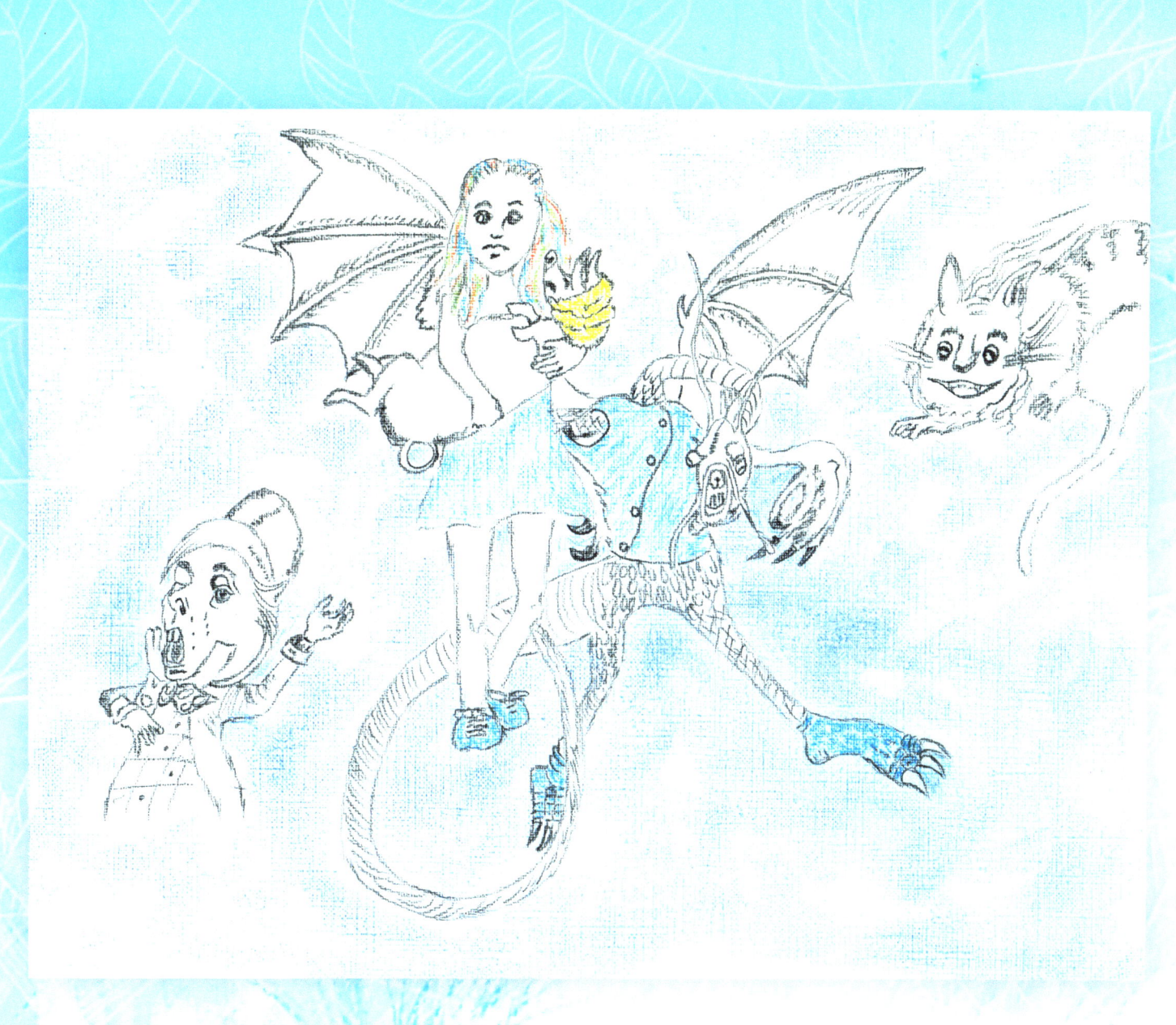

ABANDONS THE OX

The struggle is over. The mind that had been divided is brought into a state of *oneness*.

Having gone beyond the small self, we are now one with the Ox, riding home on the Ox, the phenomenal and true absolute as one . . . this is the shining of the world at oneness.

In the Universe there is a great, huge energy that gives life to all things. No matter what crisis or dilemma we might encounter, it will not last, and we return to this great universal energy.

The worlds of heaven and hell are exactly the same; the only difference is the state of mind of those living there. With a slight shift in how this world is used, it could become heaven or become hell.

And the moon emerges from the clouds sending out a single shaft of icy light from before the age of Ion.

Even with the clouds in front of it, our mind has always been bright, fully revealed, unmoved.

We abandon the Ox but the person remains. The true essence is not yet realised. That dualism has to be thrown away as well . . . we *aspire to nothing*.

Advice from a Caterpillar
The Caterpillar

"...and who are you?"
"I am Alice."
"And what is an Alice?"

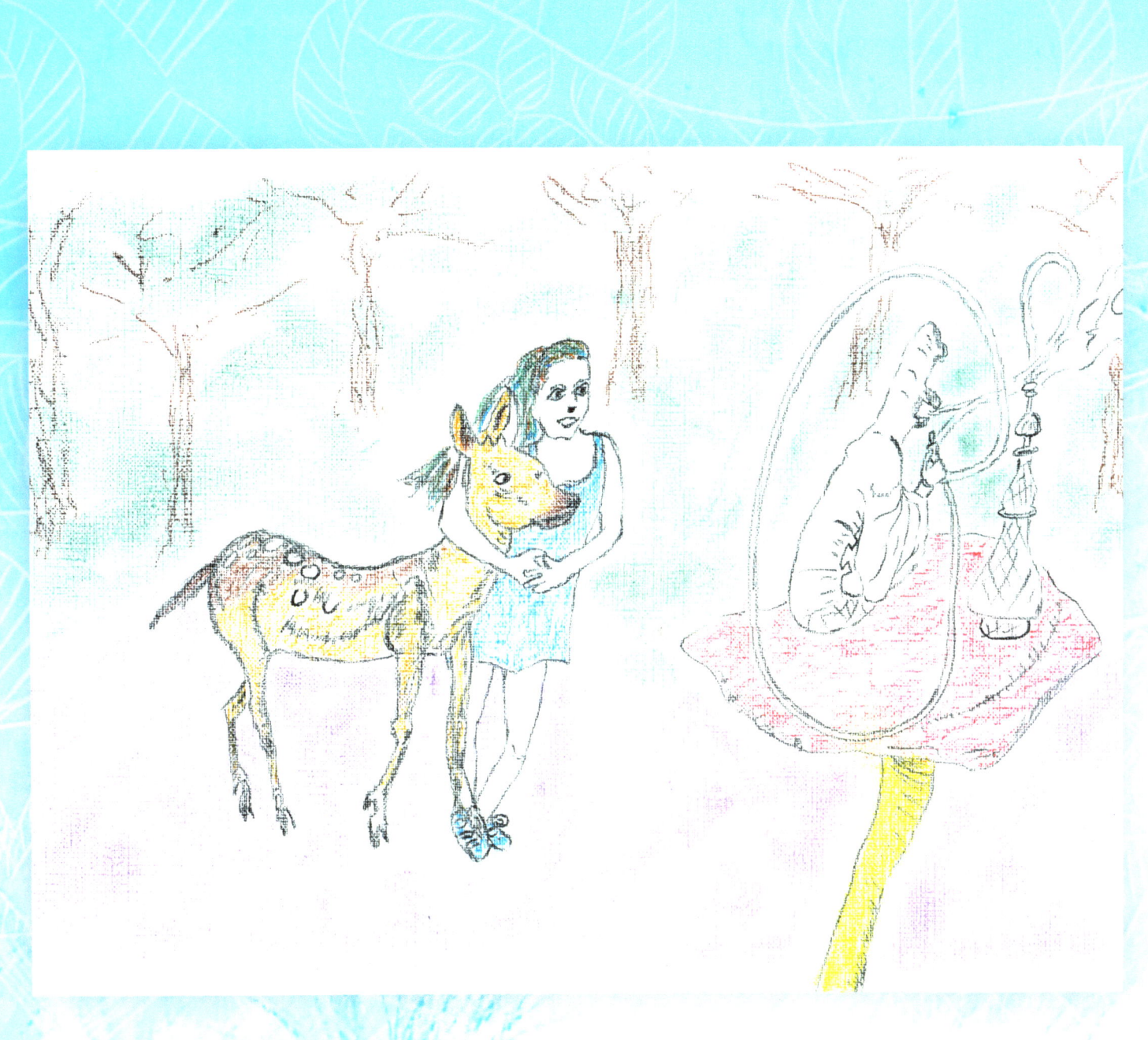

ASPIRES TO NOTHING

Whip and line, man and Ox . . . all vanished to emptiness.
All worldly feelings shed, all thought of holiness erased.
Gone all sense of separation between ourselves and others.
Only when we reach the place where all concepts of man or woman, good or bad, are completely forgotten, can we say it is a place of aspiring to nothing . . .
We must actually experience this for it to be true freedom.
The journey is to clarify our mind's essence.
From within ourselves, from within our deepest darkest mind, we decide to seek a path. We see a glimpse of the footprint of the Ox. We catch sight of the Ox. We catch the Ox itself but cannot use it freely. We tame it until we no longer become caught on small things and are free. But there is still a self who has tamed it and whom we feel is free. We become caught on this self, still.

To let go of that is to abandon the Ox and the self, the 'I'
. . . aspires to nothing.

Advice from Alice
Alice

"I am I, you are me and I am you...
we inter-are, and all is One."

22

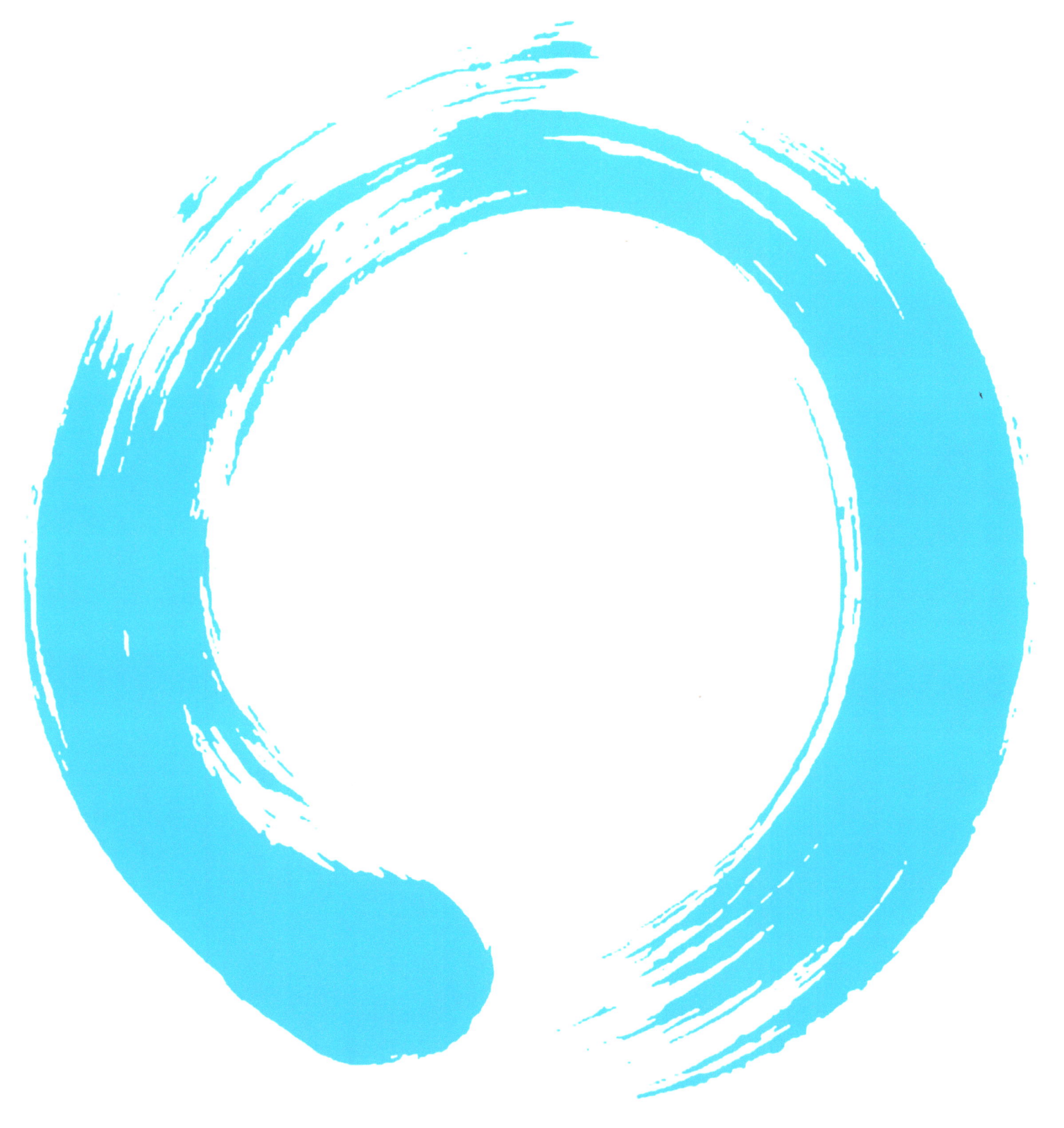

ASPIRES TO EVERYTHING

If we experience aspiring to nothing, what is then manifested is this aspiring to everything.

From that essence of holding on to nothing whatsoever, things are experienced exactly as they are, and the world that is born from that world of nothing at all, the great brilliance of all things shining, coming forth of their own . . . that is the world of 'aspires to everything'.

Return to the origin . . . back to the source . . . that state of mind which is pure as it was in the origin. Our six senses are from the origin pure.

At the age of sixteen months a child understands 'one'. At the age of thirty-two months a child understands 'two', and the ego comes forth . . . the world of duality.

Life is a maze in which we lose the way before we even learn to walk.

But the original mind is not that mind of one, but what exists prior to that, it is that world of zero.

Having let go of all of the impurities of thoughts and delusions, ideas of past and future, we are now free to experience the actual essence of each thing . . .

that deep truth.

Advice from Alice
Alice

"My journey has brought me to the gate.
Once I pass through the gate,
enlightenment is mine."

Advice from a Frog
The Frog

"The gateless way is gateless,
approached in a thousand ways.
Once past this checkpoint
you stride through the Universe."

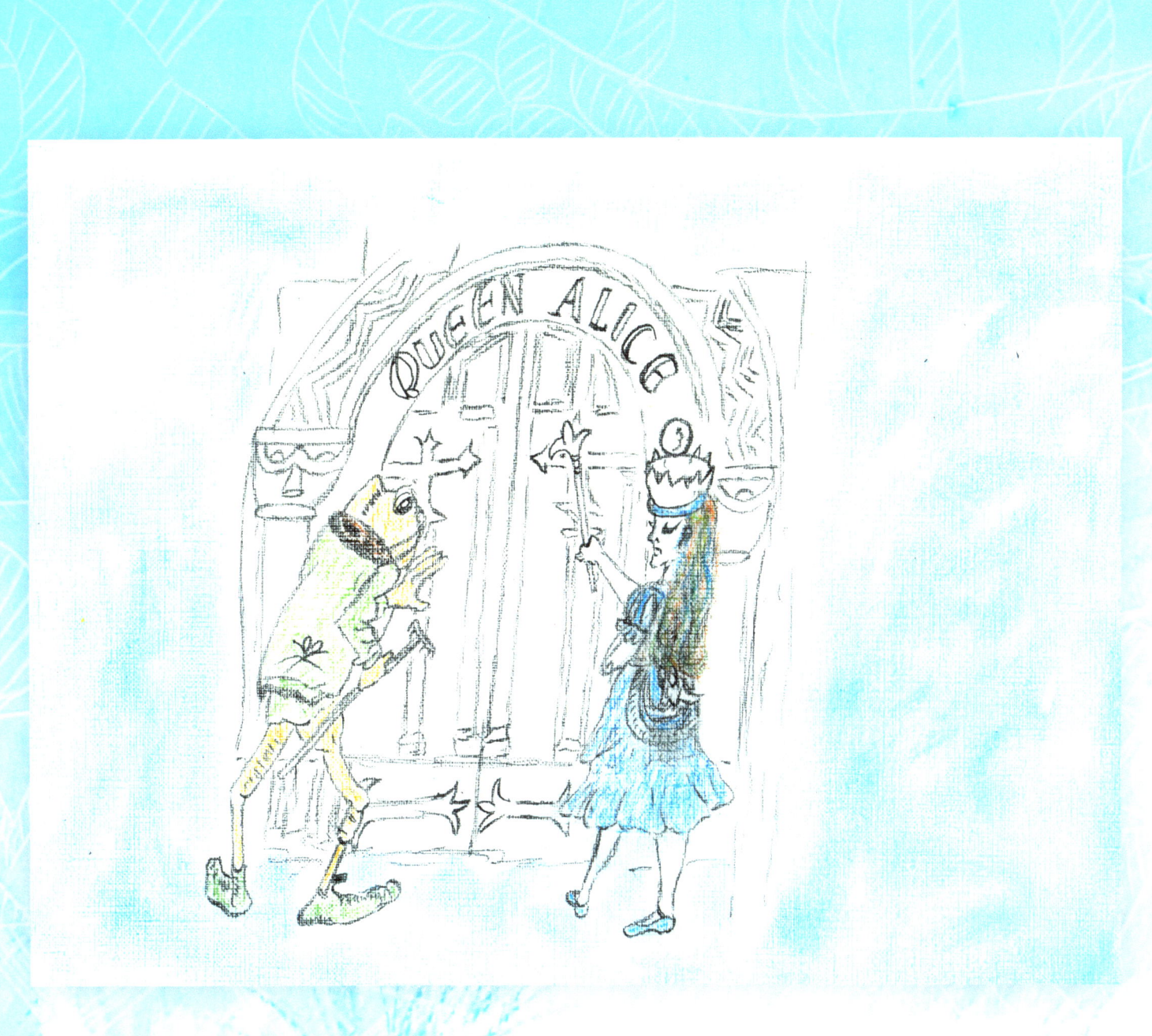

COMING DOWN FROM THE MOUNTAIN

Finally . . . down from the mountain, a big, fat, laughing Wizard carrying a huge pack.

Advice from Alice
Alice

"....it is not sufficient that I be, I must inter-be with every other thing...This is my porpoise."

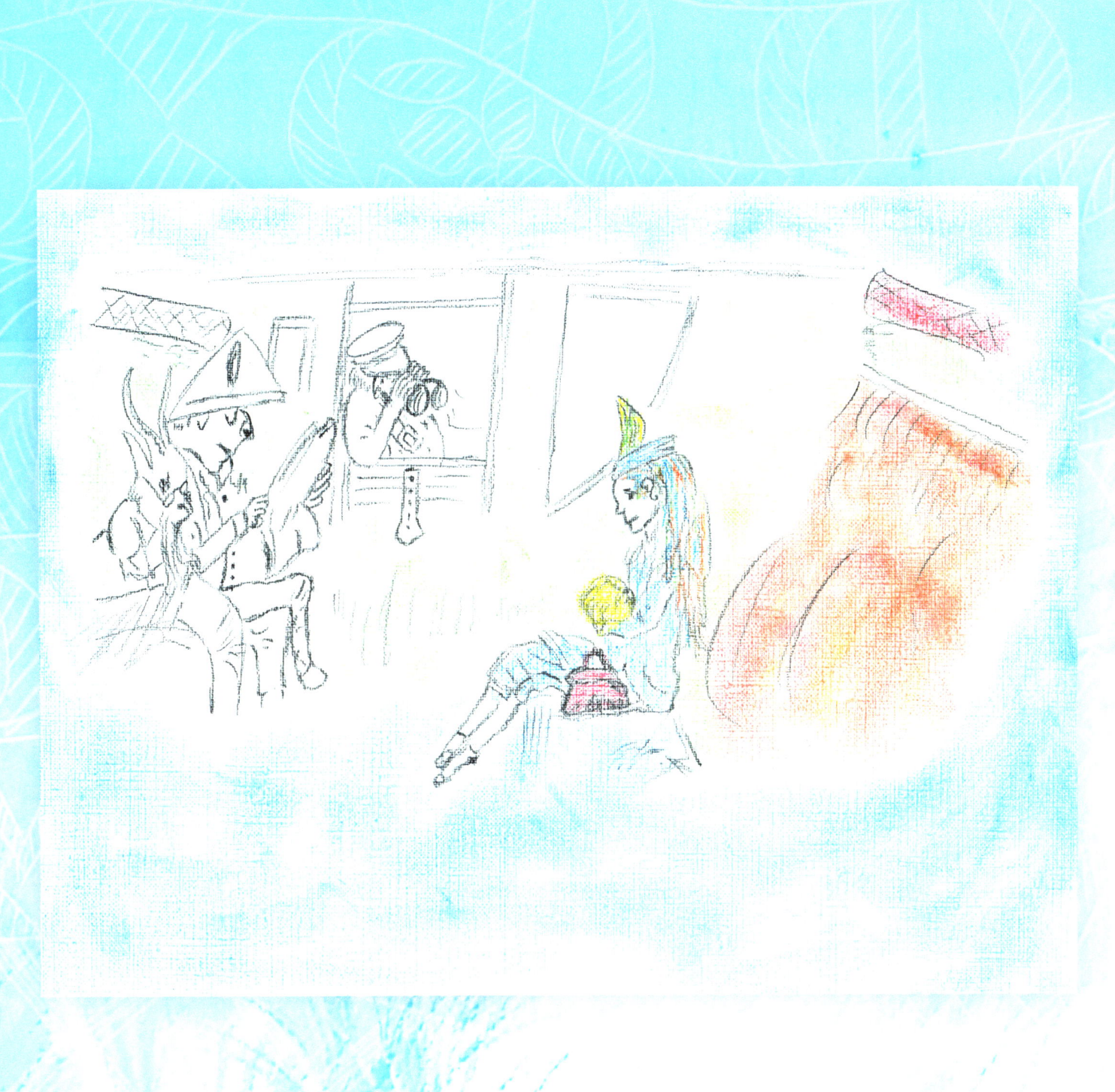

ENTERING THE MARKETPLACE

Finally . . . down from the mountain, a big fat laughing wizard carrying a huge pack, goes down to the marketplace to get drunk with the butchers. Well . . . this is one of many interpretations of this ancient Chinese classic, but for Alice, I'm sure a tea party would be far more appreciated!

In 'forgetting both person and Ox', we who have been searching for the light, are able to become, melt and enter into that light in oneness. And then in 'aspiring to everything', we return to the origin where there is only that light. We return from there and we become and reflect all the mountains and the trees and the rivers. This is the world of truth, of paradise, of loveliness where there is no prejudice and no differentiation among things. Things are exactly as they are.

Now down from our mountain, within our own mind we give light to every single thing we come in contact with.

We have realized our original pure mind, the Buddha Nature we are all born with . . . clearing up all delusion, anger and ignorance . . .

now there is only truth.

Advice from a Mad Hatter
Hatty

"What happens Alice,
when you realise enlightenment?"

Advice from Alice
Alice

"Everything changes...and nothing changes. Shall we have a cup of tea Hatty? And perhaps you might care to invite Mr Doormouse to join us."

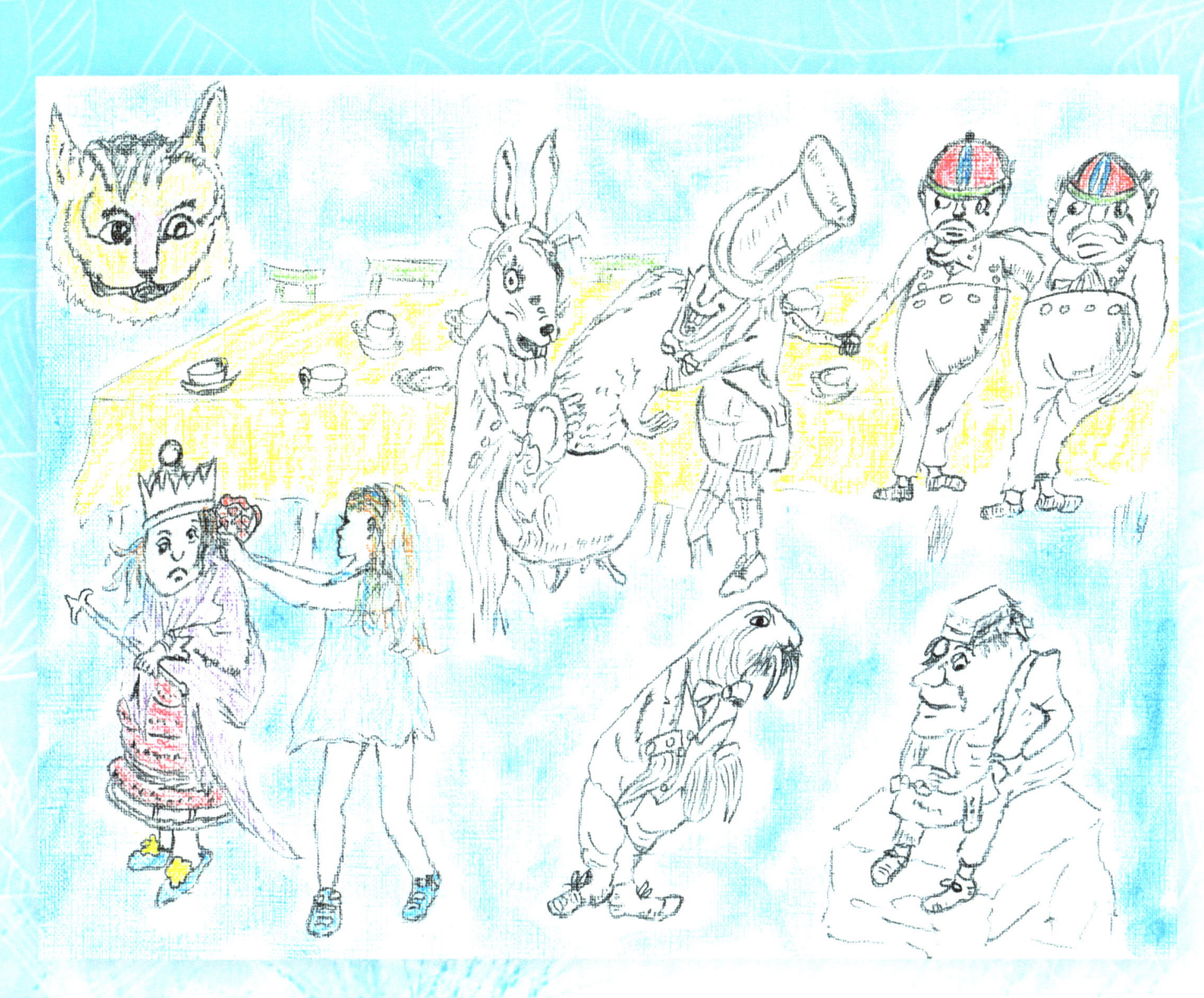

Advice from a Walrus
The Walrus

"The time has come (the Walrus said)
to talk of many things:
Of shoes - and ships - and sealing wax -
Of cabbages - and kings -
And why the sea is boiling hot -
And whether pigs have wings."

Advice from a Carpenter
The Carpenter

"I don't know. I don't care. And it doesn't make
any difference. There is nothing to be taught,
nothing to be transmitted. It is just a matter of
seeing one's own nature (enlightenment)."

Advice from a Cat
Cheshire Puss

"She who knows to stop at what she does not
know has attained the ultimate. Share your
knowledge Alice;
it is a way to achieve immortality."

Advice from a Guru
Swami Bhagawan Baba

"When the road ends and the goal is gained, the
pilgrim finds that she has travelled from
herself to herself.

Advice from the twins
Tweedledum and Tweedledee

"There is no enlightenment outside daily life."

A boat, beneath a sunny sky.
Lingering onward dreamily
In an evening of July-
Children three that nestle near,
Eager eye and willing ear,
Pleased a simple tale to hear-
Long has paled that sunny sky:
Echoes fade and memories die:
Autumn frosts have slain July.
Still she haunts me phantomwise.
Alice moving under skies
Never seen by waking eyes.
Children yet, the tale to hear,
Eager eye and willing ear
Lovingly shall nestle near.
In a Wonderland they lie
Dreaming as the days go by
Dreaming as the summers die:
Ever drifting down the stream-
Lingering in golden gleam-
Life, what is it but a dream?

Lewis Carroll

GLOSSARY OF TERMS

- Zenaholic   One who is addicted to Zen.
- Dharma Bum   The Zen Master would give me a thorough thrashing with his big stick.
- Dharma Bum Mother   Second highest Order of Dharma Bums.
- Oh Enlightened One   One solidly in the world of truth.
- Mini-Me Guru   Still a caterpillar
- Legend of the Universe   Highest Order of Legends.